Living in the
Australian Outback

Jane Bingham

www.raintreepublishers.co.uk
Visit our website to find out more information about **Raintree** books.

To order:
☎ Phone 44 (0) 1865 888112
🖹 Send a fax to 44 (0) 1865 314091
🖥 Visit the Raintree bookshop at **www.raintreepublishers.co.uk** to browse our catalogue and order online.

First published in Great Britain by
Raintree, Halley Court, Jordan Hill,
Oxford OX2 8EJ, part of Harcourt Education.
Raintree is a registered trademark
of Harcourt Education Ltd.

Editorial: Catherine Veitch
Design: Richard Parker and Manhattan Design
Illustration: International Mapping
Picture Research: Hannah Taylor and Maria Joannou
Production: Alison Parsons

Originated by Modern Age
Printed and bound in China by SCPC

ISBN 978-1 4062 0821 4
12 11 10 09 08
10 9 8 7 6 5 4 3 2 1

**British Library Cataloguing in
Publication Data**
Bingham, Jane
Living in the Australian outback. - (World cultures)
994'.07
A full catalogue record for this book is available
from the British Library.

Some of the images used in this book may have
associations with deceased Indigenous Australians.
Please be aware that these images may cause sadness
or distress in Aboriginal or Torres Strait islander
communities.

Acknowledgements
The publishers would like to thank the following for
permission to reproduce photographs: The Estate of
Clifford Possum Tjapaltijarri licensed by DACS/AAA/
VISCOPY 2007 pp. **4** (Photo: Corbis/ Penny Tweedie),
16 (Photo: Bridgeman Art Library/ Corbally Stourton
Contemporary Art, London, UK); A1Pix p. **19**; Alamy
Images pp. **26** (Machteld Baljet & Marcel Hoevenaars),
25 (Suzy Bennett); Corbis pp. **8**, **29** (Robert Harding
World Imagery), **14** (Buddy Mays), **12** (Christine
Osborne), **21**, **23** (Free Agents Limited), **18** (Herbert
Spichtinger/ Zefa), **9** (Martin Harvey; Gallo Image),
10 (Michael & Patricia Fogden), **22** (Paul Almasy), **5**
(Penny Tweedie); Eye Ubiquitous/ Hutchinson p. **15**;
Lonely Planet Images pp. **20** (Paul Dymond), **13** (Peter
Ptzchelinzew); NHPA/ ANT Photo Library pp. **24**, **28**;
Photographers Direct/ Jayawardene Travel Photo
Library p. **17**; Photolibrary/ Ifa-Bilderteam Gmbh p. **7**;
Photolibrary/Pacific Stock p. **11**; Science Photo Library/
Adrian T Sumner p. **27**.

Cover photograph of Clifford Possum on the site that
inspired this recent painting whose title is 'Love Story',
reproduced with permission of © The Estate of Clifford
Possum Tjapaltjarri licensed by DACS/AAA/VISCOPY 2007
Photo: CORBIS SYGMA/ John Van Hasselt.

Every effort has been made to contact copyright holders
of any material reproduced in this book. Any omissions
will be rectified in subsequent printings if notice is given
to the publishers.

Contents

Some words are printed in bold, **like this**. You can find out
what they mean on page 31.

Living in the outback

What is the **outback**? The outback is land in Australia far away from cities and coasts. It is also known as the **bush**.

In the outback, wild plants grow and animals roam freely. For thousands of years, the outback was also home to many Australian Aboriginal peoples.

◄ Here, the artist Clifford Possum Tjapaltjarri makes the same marks on his canvas as his **ancestors** drew on the sand thousands of years ago.

DIFFERENT NAMES

The Aboriginal people are also known as Indigenous Australians. Both these names have the same meaning. They mean that the Aboriginals were the first people to live in Australia.

▲ Many Aboriginal people still live in the outback. Most of them live in permanent camps. They usually buy their food from a community store.

The Aboriginal people

Some Aboriginal people have lived in the outback for more than 50,000 years. In the past, they had a **traditional** way of life. They hunted animals and gathered food to eat. They also had many beliefs about their land.

ABORIGINALS TODAY

Today, only a few Aboriginal people follow a traditional way of life. Some paint pictures and tell stories about their beliefs. A few still gather food from the bush.

Life in the Central Desert

Many Aboriginal people live in the Central Desert. This is an enormous, dry, sandy region. The Central Desert is in the middle of Australia. During the day the desert is scorching hot. At night it can get very cold.

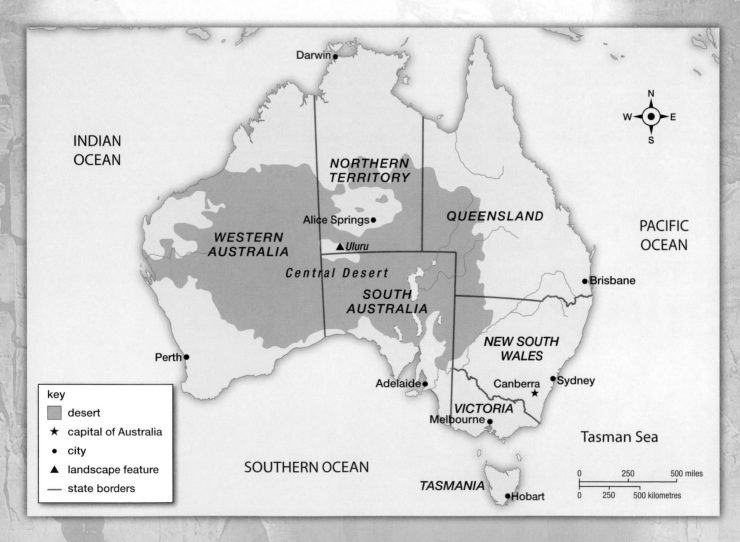

Darwin

INDIAN OCEAN

NORTHERN TERRITORY

Alice Springs

▲ Uluru

WESTERN AUSTRALIA

Central Desert

QUEENSLAND

PACIFIC OCEAN

● Brisbane

SOUTH AUSTRALIA

NEW SOUTH WALES

Perth ●

Adelaide ●

Canberra ★

● Sydney

VICTORIA

Melbourne ●

Tasman Sea

SOUTHERN OCEAN

key
- ▦ desert
- ★ capital of Australia
- ● city
- ▲ landscape feature
- — state borders

TASMANIA

● Hobart

0   250   500 miles
0   250   500 kilometres

▲ The Central Desert is just a part of the vast Australian **outback**.

Sand and rocks

In the Central Desert, there are vast **plains** of flat, sandy land. There are also hills and **ridges** made from sand. Rocks of all sizes are scattered over the landscape.

◄ The sand and rocks of the Central Desert are deep red. Aboriginal artists often use this colour in their paintings.

LAND ART

The Aboriginal people of the Central Desert make a special kind of art. They mark out large designs on the sand.

Desert plants and animals

Even though the Central Desert is very dry, it has a wide range of plants. Tough, spiny grass covers the hills and **plains**. Wattles and bush tomatoes are found on hillsides. Eucalyptus trees grow by streams. Eucalyptus trees are also called gum trees.

▲ **Witchetty grubs** live in the roots and stalks of desert plants. They can be eaten raw or cooked. Some people say they taste like prawns.

Desert creatures

The Central Desert is home to a lot of different creatures. Kangaroos and **wallabies** hop across the plains. Eagles and parrots fly overhead. Lizards and snakes lie on the rocks in the sun. There are also many desert insects, such as honey ants.

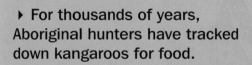
▸ For thousands of years, Aboriginal hunters have tracked down kangaroos for food.

SURVIVING IN THE OUTBACK

In the past, the Aboriginal people found everything they needed in the **outback**. Even today, they know how to survive in the outback. They can live for weeks without going near any houses or shops.

Ancestor Spirits

The Aboriginal people believe in **Ancestor Spirits**. These powerful Spirits have many different forms. Some of the Ancestor Spirits look like giant men or women. Others look like animals, insects, or plants.

Desert spirits

Each part of Australia has its own Ancestor Spirits. In the Central Desert, most of the Spirits look like desert creatures, such as lizards and snakes. The Carpet Snake Ancestors look like snakes found in the desert today.

◀ Carpet snakes live in the Central Desert. The Aboriginal people believe that these snakes were powerful spirits in the past.

▲ At sunrise and sunset, Uluru turns blood red. This reminds some people of the battle of the Carpet Snake Spirits.

THE STORY OF ULURU

Uluru is a giant rock in the heart of the Central Desert (see map on page 6). The Aboriginal people tell many stories about this rock. In one story, the Carpet Snake Spirits lived on Uluru. They fought a bloody battle to defend their rocky home. After the battle, Uluru was stained red with the Spirits' blood.

The Aboriginal people believe that the Earth was created in a time called the **Dreamtime**. This special time happened millions of years ago, but it is still remembered today.

▸ This painting is called Snake Dreaming. It shows a snake Ancestor Spirit in the desert.

DREAMING TRACKS

Each **Ancestor Spirit** made a different journey in the Dreamtime. The paths that the Spirits took are called the **dreaming tracks**. There are hundreds of dreaming tracks in the Central Desert.

▲ The Aboriginal people believe that everything in their landscape was created by Ancestor Spirits in the Dreamtime.

Dreamtime journeys

In the Dreamtime, the Ancestor Spirits travelled all over the Earth, making rocks, streams, and hills. On their journeys, the Spirits also created animals, plants, and people. Sometimes the Spirits stopped and rested on their Dreamtime journeys, and sometimes they hunted for food.

Following the dreaming tracks

For centuries, Aboriginal people have followed the **dreaming tracks** made by their **Ancestor Spirits**. Many still follow these ancient tracks today. People learn a lot about their land while they are following the dreaming tracks.

◀ Older people teach younger people about the dreaming tracks.

▲ This painting shows some of the dreaming tracks that the Aboriginal people believe cover the Australian landscape.

Remembering the journey

Aboriginal people hold special ceremonies to celebrate the dreaming tracks. They sing songs and tell stories. This helps them to remember everything that happened on the Spirit's journey during the **Dreamtime**.

They remember the places where a Spirit rested or drank from a stream. They also remember the places where a Spirit went hunting. This knowledge helps them learn the best way to use their land.

Aboriginal artists often paint pictures of the **dreaming tracks**. This helps them to remember the journeys of the **Ancestor Spirits**. The paintings look like maps of the land.

▶ This painting is called **Dingo** Dreaming. It shows the dreaming track of the Dingo Ancestor Spirit. Dingos are wild dogs that live in the desert. Can you see the Dingo Spirit's paw prints?

Old and new

In the past, Aboriginal artists used natural colours for their paintings. They made these colours from ground-up rocks. Today, many artists use modern paints. But they still paint **traditional** subjects.

▼ This painting was made by an artist in northern Australia.

READING THE SIGNS

The paintings of the dreaming tracks are full of signs. These signs can have more than one meaning. A circle can mean a campsite or a well. A semicircle may mean a person sitting down or a **boomerang**. Some of the signs in a painting are secret. Only the Aboriginal people know what they mean.

Music and dance

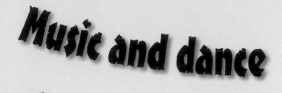

Music and dance are very important to the Aboriginal people. They sing **traditional** songs and perform special dances. The songs and dances tell the stories of the **Dreamtime**. There are also special ceremonies for the dead.

▶ Sometimes Aboriginal people play modern musical instruments. This man plays a guitar. But he still sings about his ancient beliefs.

CORROBOREES

Many ceremonies are sacred and secret. But some music and dances are performed for the public. These public performances are usually known as **corroborees**.

▸ This man is playing clap sticks at a corroboree.

Making music

Aboriginal ceremonies do not just involve singing and dancing. The Aboriginal people also make music for the dancers. They use different instruments in different parts of Australia. In the Central Desert, people clap special sticks together. These sticks are known as **clap sticks**.

Body decoration

Today, Aboriginal people wear modern clothes. But they dress differently for dances and ceremonies. During dances and ceremonies, they decorate their bodies in a **traditional** way.

▲ The colours used for body decoration are made from earth and white clay.

Patterns and ornaments

Dancers use natural **pigments** to paint bold patterns on their faces and bodies. These patterns are different for each family group. The older people teach the patterns to the young. They explain the special meanings of the patterns.

Men and women dancers wear ornaments. These ornaments include **pendants**, belts, and armbands. They are made from natural materials, such as bones. They can also be made from feathers and berries.

▲ Some Aboriginal men decorate their bodies before they go hunting.

BODY MAPS

Sometimes, the patterns on a man's body represent the land of his people. They can show **symbols** of rocks, trees, and streams.

Hunting in the outback

For thousands of years, Aboriginal people hunted animals such as kangaroos and emus (large birds). They also hunted lizards, snakes, and other small creatures. Today, some Aboriginal people still go hunting. They mainly use guns to kill their **prey**.

◄ Some hunters use a curved stick called a **boomerang**. They throw the boomerang at their prey. Some boomerangs are specially made so that they return to the thrower.

▸ This hunter is using a long, wooden spear. He aims very carefully before he throws it at his prey.

SPEARS AND BOOMERANGS

In the past, desert hunters used wooden weapons. They hurled long spears at their prey. They also threw boomerangs at birds and other creatures. Sometimes hunters worked in teams to track down a group of animals.

Spear throwers

Traditional hunters used **spear throwers** to help them throw their spears. The spear thrower was a simple lever. When the hunter was ready to shoot, he released his spear. With the help of a spear thrower, spears can travel up to 90 metres (300 feet).

Gathering food

For centuries, the Aboriginal people found all their food in the **outback**. Nowadays they can buy their food in shops. But some still find food in the **bush**.

HONEY ANTS

People in the desert get their honey from ants. Honey ants usually live in nests under the ground. Women find the nests. Then they dig up the ants.

▲ Honey ants have huge stomachs. They store honey inside their stomachs.

▲ The flowers of the Honey Grevillia contain a sweet juice, called **nectar**. Aboriginal people suck the nectar from these flowers. Sometimes they dip the flowers in water to make a sweet drink.

Finding food

In the past, Aboriginal men and women had different jobs. Men went hunting and women gathered food. The women picked fruit from bushes. They also gathered nuts and seeds. They used digging sticks to dig up desert **yams** and wild potatoes.

Making medicines

In the past, Aboriginal people used plants or animals to make their medicines. Today, some still make **traditional** medicines. Here are a few examples.

Helpful trees

Eucalytpus trees have many uses. Their leaves can be mixed with boiling water. This makes a **disinfectant** to put on wounds. Strips of the soft bark also make very good bandages. The ghost gum is a kind of eucalyptus tree. **Sap** from its trunk makes a soothing **ointment** for aching muscles.

▸ The ghost gum tree gets its name from its ghostly white bark colour.

NO MORE WARTS!

The spines of the prickly wattle bush can get rid of warts. The spines are pushed into the base of the wart. After about a week, the wart becomes very dry. Then the wart drops off.

▲ The prickly moses plant belongs to the same family as the prickly wattle.

Curing colds

The apple bush provides good cures for colds. Sniffing its flowers helps to clear a blocked nose. Some Aboriginal people also make an ointment from its leaves. They grind up some leaves and mix them with animal fat. Then they rub the ointment on their chest to help them breathe more easily.

How would you survive in the outback?

For thousands of years, the Aboriginal people found everything they needed in the desert. How would you manage in the **outback**? Try this quiz to find out.

1. If you saw a **witchetty grub,** would you...
   A   Run away screaming?
   B   Rub it on your chest?
   C   Enjoy it as a tasty snack?

2. What would you use as a **disinfectant** to put on wounds?
   A   Honey Grevillia flowers
   B   Eucalyptus leaves
   C   White clay

3. Where do honey ants store honey?
   A   Inside a tree
   B   Under a leaf
   C   Inside their stomachs

▸ This is a honey ant.

4. *What would you do with the spines of a prickly wattle bush?*

A Cook them as a soup
B Grind them up to make an **ointment**
C Use them to get rid of warts

5. *Which of these foods would you find with a digging stick?*

A Bush tomatoes
B Desert **yams**
C **Wallabies**

◄ These are witchetty grubs.

Books to read

Aboriginal People Then and Now: Sharing our Cultures, Alex Barlow and
      Marji Hill (Heinemann Library, Melbourne, 2001)
Australian Library: Desert Dreamings, Deirde Stoke
      (Heinemann Library, Melbourne, 2004)

Websites

www.aboriginalaustralia.com/
A website run by Aboriginal people. It includes sections on art and music.

www.dreamtime.net.au
This large website includes stories told by Aboriginal people.

www.mjhall.org/bushtucker/index.htm
A guide to food from the bush, written by Aboriginal children from the
Central Desert.

Glossary

ancestor relative, such as a great-grandparent, from a long time before

Ancestor Spirit kind of god for the Aboriginal people. They believe that the Ancestor Spirits created Earth and all living things.

boomerang heavy, curved stick used for hunting animals and birds

bush land in Australia far away from cities and coasts

clap sticks wooden sticks that are banged together to make a noise

corroboree ceremony performed for the public

dingo wild dog that lives in the outback of Australia

disinfectant something you put on wounds to kill germs

dreaming tracks tracks across the landscape that were made by the Ancestor Spirits

Dreamtime time when Earth was created by the Ancestor Spirits

nectar sweet liquid that bees collect from flowers and turn into honey

ointment kind of paste that is put on wounds or rubbed on the chest

outback land in Australia far away from cities and coasts

pendant ornament that is hung on a string around the neck

pigment paint or dye, usually made from natural materials

plain large, level area of land

prey creature that is hunted

ridge raised piece of land

sap liquid inside plants and trees

spear thrower lever that hunters use to help them throw their spears. A spear thrower is also known as a woomera.

symbol mark or picture that means something else

traditional done the same way for a very long time

Uluru very large rock in the Central Desert region of Australia

wallaby Australian animal that looks like a small kangaroo

witchetty grub caterpillar that lives in the Australian outback

yam vegetable that grows underground in hot countries

Index